What Will Happen in 2012 and Beyond?

Eloheim and The Council

Channeled by Veronica Torres

Eloheim.com

ISBN: 978-1-936969-16-6

Copyright 2011 Veronica Torres

Published by Rontor Presents

Cover Art by Holly's Creative Design

hollyscreative.com

Mary T. George, interior design

epubpub.com

Contents

Introduction

The question, "What will happen in 2012?" is being asked by a great many people. The interest in 2012 came about because the Mayan calendar ends on 21st December 2012. Unsurprisingly, this has given rise to a considerable amount of speculation about what might happen, including predictions that the world will either end or that we will experience some sort of catastrophic event.

The end of the world has been predicted time and time again and many of the dates on which this was supposed to happen have come and gone. Since we have difficulty accurately predicting the weather for even a few days ahead, is it likely that we will be able to predict something like the end of the world?

Some of the end of the world warnings you will find online and elsewhere are based on biblical prophesies. For those who take the Bible literally, recent natural events such as earthquakes and tsunamis, as well as the global economic crisis may be interpreted as proof of various end-of-the-world prophecies in the Bible. These events have led to many people, irrespective

of their religious beliefs, to fear that something cataclysmic is
going to happen soon.

With so much fear surrounding the 2012 question, we decided to
ask Eloheim for their views on 2012. We drew up a list of commonly asked questions, based on questions typically asked on
the internet and also questions from those who follow Eloheim's
teachings.

As you are reading Eloheim's answers, you will find words and
concepts that are underlined. The underlined items are links to
more detailed information and explanations. In four cases, the
underlined items will take you to a description of an Eloheim
tool. Eloheim has given us more than 100 different tools de-
signed to support healing and facilitate the transformation of
fears, habits, and unconscious areas of our lives.

You can learn more about Eloheim's tools in our books *The Choice
for Consciousness, Tools for Conscious Living* and the companion
series, *The Homo Spiritus Sessions*. Details about the books are
listed at the end of this book.

Questions

Mayans

***What did the Mayans know about 2012 and why does their
calendar end in December of 2012?***
The Mayans made a lot of astrological observations. They looked
up in the sky and they made astrological observations just like
you do. What is today? The first day of summer. You made an
astrological observation. What happens in your calendar round
about this time of year? All the kids stop going to school. How
did you know the kids were supposed to stop going to school?
Well, because it's true. You guys make decisions; you format
time. December 25th, that's a holiday. July 4th, that's a holiday.
You have these preconceived notions about the way you format
time. The Mayans had a way of formatting time, they based it on
astrological observations, and they extrapolated this calendar out
many thousands of years.

Why does it end? It's a cycle of their calendar that concludes.
It would be like you asking, "Why does my calendar end on
December 31st?" Because it does; that's how you have formatted

time. Even if your calendar lasts 25,000 years, at some point, you get to the equivalent of December 31st. At some point you get to it.

The idea that 2012 is the end point of the Mayan calendar or the changeover of the Mayan calendar is noticed very strongly because it seems kind of drastic. You also wonder, "What the heck happened to the Mayans, anyway?" The mystery of the Mayans and 2012 wouldn't be a mystery if the Mayans were still around because the Mayans would tell you what is going to happen the day after their calendar ends. After all, they're the ones that created the calendar. But they're not here anymore so it gives you guys a big opportunity for speculation. The great thing is that it has caused an energetic uprising or an energetic attention point and that's really the part that's fascinating to us.

When you guys have a special event on your calendar, whether it is the change of month or a change of year, there's an energetic associated with the focus you are putting on that specific time that we can work with to help you grow and transform. When there's a holiday we can work with the fact that you, as a society, have set aside a specific energetic for that time of year. We can work with the fact that it's warm. We can work with the fact that it's cold. We can work with the fact that the kids got out of school or didn't get out of school. The focus you have placed on 2012 is a similar energetic attention point.

Hopi

Why did the Hopi point to 2012 and say any chance at salvation is now useless as we have gone too far?

Well, you really have to ask the Hopi about that. We would suggest that if this is something that really concerns you, you go find a Hopi elder and you sit at his/her feet and learn why the Hopi viewpoint and construction of time is so bleak. We believe that it is most likely because their way of life is not being honored. The way they live is not being honored. If you were of a Christian background you could say, "Why are so few people celebrating Christmas and Easter?" If you feel these days are not being celebrated properly you could feel like your way of life is dying. You could say very easily, "If you don't celebrate Easter and Christmas properly, there's no hope for you." People say that. We are bringing the Hopi's concept into a culture that you're more familiar with so that you can see that it's not just the Hopi saying this; there are other cultures saying this when they don't feel their important traditions are honored.

Now again, the Hopi and the Mayans are given a place in a lot of people's minds as being very wise and having lots to teach the "white man" and to contribute wisdom that you don't feel you have. But you have to remember, they're bringing wisdom from their perspective. Does their perspective resonate as a perspective you want to adopt? If it does, then follow the whole thing. Don't just pick one little teaching or one little line of information out of their entire culture and then fixate on it. Doing so is likely to cause you suffering.

Fear

Why is there so much fear about 2012?

Most people live in fear all the time. They're lots and lots of things to fear and the main reason why there are lots of things to fear is the survival instinct is constantly looking for dangers to avoid in order to keep you alive. You've been taught to live by looking out for things you need to be afraid of and looking for danger.

A lot of the fear around 2012 comes from folks taking individual pieces of different cultures and interpreting their predictions in a way that supports the fears from which most people live. When you look at the Hopi or the Mayans or whomever else is predicting that there's a calamity coming in 2012, it's another very large thing to potentially be afraid of.

Just like going out of the house or getting on an airplane or getting in your car can frighten you because it's potentially dangerous, so can the idea that maybe these people know that there's something really big "I should be afraid of." You're really, really trained to be afraid very easily and very profoundly.

Helping you move out of the fear-based operating system is a major focus of our teachings.

Disasters

Isn't it pretty likely there will be one or more disasters in the future?

What is a "disaster"? Is a disaster spilling red wine on your white pants? Is a disaster one of your children dying young? Is a disaster your house burning down? Is a disaster someone breaking up with you? Is a disaster a bad hair day on an important interview day? Floods, famines, earthquakes, tornadoes, tsunamis, hurricanes—a lot of people think those are disasters, especially when they're happening to you.

Is there going to be a disaster in 2012?

Define disaster for yourself first and then see the likelihood of it. There's going to be an earthquake, there's going to be a hurricane, there's going to be a tsunami and typhoon, and there's probably going to be all kinds of other things like that. Is that because it's 2012 or is that because that's part of the human experience? We would vote it's part of the human experience.

Is it true that the Earth's population will be reduced to 500 million?

No.

Jesus

Will Jesus reappear in 2012?

Couldn't tell you. That's up to Jesus.

Aliens

Will aliens rescue the surviving population like a modern Noah's ark?

We really want to talk about the alien thing because there's a lot of energy around, "We're going to be saved by the aliens." Now, we believe anything is possible and we believe 100 percent that you have free will to create your reality. Will some people experience the idea that something alien will come and change their life? Probably. Because we believe that strongly in your ability to create your reality. We also believe that this entire Earth journey was predicated on the idea of free will. The idea that you've expressed your free will and then some outside force has to come in and change your experience in order to "save" you from your problems or "save" you from your screw-ups makes absolutely no sense to us. That does not sit well with how we understand this place to work. From our perspective, the idea that the aliens are going to come and bring you peace, bring you whatever you think they're going to bring you, is not likely. You are here to grow. You are here to transform. You are here to become something new.

Now, we've had some experience working with people and what we know is you can't tell them a damn thing and you can't force them and you certainly cannot make something that's not their idea happen, period. We don't even have to include free will in that. We just say you're stubborn. You don't like being told what to do. The idea that an alien race would come to this planet and tell you what to do and you would like it? Right away that confuses us. And some people say, "Oh, but they'll fix all our problems." The only thing we've ever seen you guys all agree on is breathing. There's only one thing we've always had you guys agree on and that's that you're willing to breathe. So what are your problems and how should they be fixed and how will the aliens know what you need done and will you all agree that the alien's plan is the "right" plan, etc.?

Additionally, you have a cultural bias brought on by your science fiction books and movies that says, "When the aliens come, things get bad. Even if the aliens start out 'nice,' they don't stay that way." This bias would have an effect on any potential encounters with aliens.

We just cannot see large scale alien encounters being a constructive worldwide event.

Now, does that mean you are the only life forms in the galaxy? Absolutely not. Does that mean that the other ones out there are going to come over here and mess around with your free will and muck around in your planet and tell you you've been bad and wrong and you have to be fixed? That's not how we see it going down.

Are aliens already here? The Earth is a free-will zone; so if aliens try to interfere, is there some sort of protection for Earth, somebody to step in and say, "That's Earth. It's a free will zone. You can't do that."?

The universe is a vast place. Almost everything you can imagine happens regularly, especially because you guys are coming from the perspective of the limited human mind. The brain is a fantastic organ, but quite limited when you consider the vastness of the soul and the vastness of the universe. So, could it happen? Everything can and will happen, most likely. That's the point of this entire exploration. Is Earth set aside as a free-will zone where everybody knows that a certain kind of thing is going on and are you in the backwater of the galaxy hidden off in a corner kind of anyway? Yeah, you're all that. So for the "aliens" to decide that Earth is the place they want to come and muck around in, well, they've got a lot more space to fool around in. You're not that special in that way. If aliens want to go alien around, they can alien around in other places. You are doing something very, very important with the ascension process and with ensouling the body and with realizing the Homo spiritus nature. That's very important and it's attractive and it's interesting, but it's not for mucking around in.

Now, when you say the aliens are already here, if you mean entities who are not human are able to observe what's going on on your planet, of course, that would be souls. And aliens, what are they? Embodied souls doing a different kind of costume-wearing. At the end of it all, you are souls having a journey and you've done many things and you will do many things in the exploration of that journey. Most of the time we see the questions of, "Will it, if it, could it?" happening when people don't want to live in what they're actually living in. You'll have plenty of time for "Will it, if it, could it?" when you're no longer being human. But while you're being human we encourage you to actually explore and enjoy and have the full experience of being human. The, "Will it, if it, could it?" can wait. You'll be much more prepared to have a full and complete experience of, "Will it, if it, could it?" when you're not being human because you will be experiencing the completeness of your soul and its vast ability to process information.

Comment: I like the idea that aliens are souls wearing different costumes, but for the purposes of the question, people envision aliens as visitors from other societies.

Instead of calling them aliens then—because even the word aliens means "foreign, not like me, different than me," and it can bring up a lot of this sci-fi energy of, "Are they good aliens or bad aliens?" and of course that all needs to be defined—what if we just referred to them as souls wearing a different costume or souls having a different experience than being human. Souls having a non-human experience. Because you're souls. And we'll tell you right now that you're only using a small percentage of your soul to run a human body. It doesn't take much of a soul to run the human form. It really doesn't. It takes a very small amount, actually. There's a big portion of your soul doing other stuff right now. So, you're an alien. You are your own alien. If you want to look at it that way, it's true. It's a perfectly reasonable way to say it. You are your own alien. And of course, that conversation could go a lot of different directions. And we won't take them there now. But it's still a fact. You are also an alien.

New Earth

It's been said that the Earth will be like a cell dividing in two—people who ascend going with the new Earth and the others staying behind thinking the rest are dead or gone.

Yes, some people will ascend first. But, you've got to be really, really careful about this word ascension because it has in it the idea that you're going to go up, as in levitation. This is not what ascension means. You also have the Christian idea of rapture, which is to go up and away leaving people behind.

Don't confuse rapture and ascension. Rapture and ascension are not the same subject. With ascension you are actually coming more fully into the physical form; you're not leaving the physical form. Ascension is a very different way to experience Earth and being human.

Students of consciousness are already living a different life than they did before they started living consciously. They have a very different life than many of the people they know. So you could say they already live in a different Earth. People who don't study consciousness primarily live as victims and they feel like the world is out to get them, that they can't catch a break, and that

everything happens against them, etc. A student of consciousness could have the exact same set of circumstances happen and
see it as a perfectly great learning opportunity.

Comment: To clarify, from a casual observer viewpoint, you
could have 20 people in a room, 10 who are ascended and 10 who
aren't, and if someone walked in they'd say, "There are 20 people
in the room." They don't look any different from each other.

What we see happening is this: Let's say you have 10 people in
the room that are living from the consciousness-based operating
system, walking the Homo spiritus path, and are living from an
ascended state. You also have 10 people in the room who have
been living from the fear-based operating system, don't realize
that they create their reality, and are following the victim path.

There are two things we anticipate happening. The first is that
people walking into the room will notice the people who are like
them. If they're living a victim path, they'll be more drawn to interact with the "victim" people. The consciousness-based people
may not even be very noticeable to them; they could kind of be
like artwork on the wall—part of the room, but not something
to engage with. Additionally, the people in the room together
may not notice each other. If you're living from a Homo spiritus
perspective, you don't want to hang out with victims and victims often don't understand people living from the Homo spiritus perspective; it can be like oil and water. Not that anyone's
wrong, you have free will to choose any path. They're just oil and
water; they don't mix.

The second thing, which is actually already starting to happen, is
that when you start living from the Homo spiritus perspective,
you will see more in your world. You notice more, you feel more,
you will be aware of more, you will have your soul's perspective on line, you will be tapping into your alternative expressions—which are past and future lifetimes—you may even be

downloading information out of the Akashic Records. From a Homo spiritus perspective you will see much, much more filling up the space, asking for your attention, and offering you insight. This can definitely feel like living on a "new Earth."

Nuclear war or asteriod

Will there be a nuclear war or will the Earth be hit by an asteroid causing an ice age?

Nuclear war and ice ages could happen. They could happen tomorrow. They could happen 10,000 years from now. They're possibilities. You have nuclear bombs. Is it likely that because the calendar arrives at 2012 all of a sudden the nuclear bombs are all going to go off even though you guys have managed not to light them off for quite a number of decades now? Unlikely. You have to remember, you may have a lot of hatred and anger towards certain groups of people—the "enemy"—but you have a stronger survival instinct. That's why the nuclear bombs haven't gone off yet. The survival instinct is stronger than hatred. Survival instinct is the bottom line. Everybody who has their finger on the button knows that if they push the button it can't be taken back. The survival instinct is very active in those decisions. They also know that if they start lighting off nuclear bombs it may be the end. The survival instinct has strong energy in there. We do not see a large-scale nuclear holocaust happening. Could it happen that one or two might, in isolation, be detonated? If it did happen, the worldwide outrage would be so strong, we believe at this time, that it would put the kibosh on the whole thing real fast.

Are you going to get hit by an asteroid? Again, highly unlikely. Certainly possible. But highly, highly unlikely. When we say certainly possible you have to understand that we make allowances for every possibility to honor your free will. When we say highly unlikely we mean that there's a very, very small possibility, but we still allow for a possibility to exist due to free will. We don't see a big collision with your planet coming because then you would need a new planet. Creating a planet isn't like just throwing out the aluminum cans and getting more at the grocery store. Planets are a little hard to come by these days, especially planets that are habitable for you guys. We don't exactly think it makes sense to trash this one with a big rock hitting it. We want you guys to have a place to grow as souls. This is a good place. A lot of thought went into making it for you.

If you're worried about a big nuclear explosion or if you're worried about some big asteroid hitting your planet and blowing it up, we ask, what is it about what's right here in your lap that you are so uncomfortable with that that's what you're fixated on instead? Let's identify that and then work together to make what's in your lap less triggering for you so that you can enjoy being in the human body and you can enjoy having the human experience of ensouling.

Pole shifts

Are pole shifts occurring that may cause chaos in 2012? How about solar flares and problems related to that causing Earth disturbance?

You have to remember that the solar flares thing is part of your cycle. Solar flares, the movement of the moon and the stars and the planets and all that, that's part of it. Will solar flares disrupt the way you live? Solar flares are going to have some interaction. But again, it's been happening forever, it's going to keep happening forever, it's part of the sun expressing the sun's relationship to the Earth, it's not just because it's 2012 that you're going to have some kind of solar flare hell happen. You are more and more dependent on technology, which interacts with solar flares in unexpected ways, so you will notice them more. Your better technology allows you to detect that they're there, but they've been going on for a long, long time.

Because you're living more consciously and raising your vibration, you can become more aware of things like solar flares. If you were just busy staying alive and growing your own food and having to hunt your own meat your attitude would likely be, "Solar flares, shmoler flares, I gotta feed my kid." It's an indication of the advancement of your society that you to even care about such things and it's an indication of the advancement of your society that you even notice them because you have technology that can register those changes.

The pole shift thing is something that's been talked about for a long time. Your Earth is undergoing her own evolution, but again, we do not see any changes happening on the Earth becoming so disastrous as to wipe out the population. That does not seem to be part of the plan for the reasons we've stated earlier and for the reasons of, "How does that help you grow as a soul to all of a sudden just be wiped out?" If you want to experience just all of a sudden being wiped out, you can have that free will experience without the rest of the planet being destroyed. There are flood areas, and earthquake areas, and volcano areas, you can have the "be wiped out experience" that way. But to wipe out the whole planet and have to start over again? We just can't see why that would be a good idea and we don't feel like energetically it's going to happen because it doesn't make sense with the plan. Which is, the plan to give you the opportunity to grow as souls through using free will, in density and in duality.

Everyone is worried about disasters on some level because the survival instinct says these might be things you have to worry about, but if they're extremely worrying to you what we always recommend is that you inquire as to what it is about your life that you're ignoring or overlooking in order to fixate on these other things. In our experience there's something right there in your lap, it's like the elephant in the room, that you don't want to look at and you're using the energy of these other potentials to distract you from attending to it.

Middle-Earth

Is it true that a civilization will emerge from middle-Earth in 2012?

There's life in the middle of the planet and it doesn't look like you because you can't live in the middle of your planet. Of course there's life there. Because there's life everywhere. There is an error in perception that we see very frequently when you talk about life. The error is that life must be like you. Or it has to be life that you recognize. You are locked into a perspective and a sensory apparatus because you've chosen to be human at this time. On a soul level, what defines life? In our book life is defined by growth—physical, spiritual, and emotional growth.

Life that a soul would recognize as life takes on an infinite number of forms. Is there life all through your planet having different experiences? Of course. And is some of that living in middle-Earth? Of course. Would you pass up the opportunity to live in middle Earth if you could? You're curious enough right now about just about anything that if we said to you, "If you want, a part of you can go live in the molten center of your Earth and it's not going to be any skin off your nose, not going to cost you any extra energy, not going to cost you any money, we could just right now wiggle our nose and a little part of your awareness would go live in the molten center of the Earth," the hands going up from people wanting to sign up would cause a wave of air that would knock us off our chair.

HERE'S AN EXAMPLE. One time we were doing a private session and we told the person that part of his soul was currently riding the light from a star across the universe. Who wants to do that, too? Hands up! Everybody wants to do that. So, you're all doing that, too. Why? Because it just takes a smidgeon of your soul to do it!

It's a little bit like setting up a webcam. Like when you have kids and you put up a little camera in the nursery so when you're on your computer you can see if the baby's doing okay, how much energy does it take to glance over periodically at the webcam? Nearly zero. So we think it's easy to imagine that your soul has little "webcams" all over the place doing all kinds of interesting things like living in the middle of the Earth.

Now, is a human figure going to walk out of the middle of the Earth and say, "I've been living in the middle of the Earth and it's 2012 so I have come out"? Well, one, we doubt it, strongly, but we don't ever say no, but we doubt it strongly, and two, you wouldn't believe them, and three, they could try to prove it to you and you wouldn't believe that, most of you, and the ones that did believe it would be called crazy by all the rest of them that didn't believe it and then someone would probably get shot. This is your nature. This is your nature. As embarrassing and giggly and as, "Oh God, that's true," as it is, that's your nature. It's rare for you to stand up and want to declare the truth of you in this moment. Can you imagine trying to declare the truth of you living down in the middle of the planet? You see how these things kind of fall apart when you look at them a little more deeply.

Some people may say, "But, but, but, Eloheim, I really believe that people live down there and they look just like us." Okay, when you meet one, have the experience of meeting them. But are you fixated on it? And if you are fixated on it, decide why. Would you rather be living in the center of the Earth? Is there something about the big open spaces that makes you feel triggered? Probably. There's a reason for your fixations. We'd love for you guys to get fixated on things just because you're curious and it makes you grow. The kind of fixation we are less excited about is siphoning off your attention to something else so you don't have to focus on what's true now. We want you to be fascinated by your own inner stuff.

We like to say, is it fear or fascination? Let's take your fears and turn them into fascination.

Overpopulation

Is overpopulation going to cause a disaster in 2012?

Population ideals come from cultural beliefs that having a bunch of kids is the right way to live. Most of you in the westernized world go, "Oh my God, we use so many resources individually we better not have a bunch of kids or we're really going to tap out the planet." Keep in mind, other people who are less resource-intensive can have a bunch of kids and still use less than your family of four uses. They can have 10 in their family and not use as much as your family of four uses. So you have to look at it from the perspective of, "Is this based on what I think the planet is undergoing or is it based on how I think people should structure their family?"

See, it all comes down to definition, you can't assume everybody knows what you're talking about and you can't assume that what you see is what other people see. Everyone is having an individual, unique experience of the world even if they're having the exact same experience. You change so quickly that you can have the exact same experience three days apart and have a completely different journey through it the second time. You have to really watch definitions and you have to really watch when you define something to not assume that everyone is defining it the same way. That's why we're very careful about the language we use and we define things a lot so that you know what we mean by a word that we use.

Is there overpopulation? The question that is more interesting is, "What about resource management?" To us that's a more accurate way of stating, "I'm concerned about management of the planet's resources." Okay, great. Will people become more concerned about that? People are becoming more concerned about that. People recycle and they compost and they want the paint that doesn't smell and they want the hybrid cars. So, people are. Is it going fast enough for your peace of mind? And again, we would say, are you going fast enough for your peace of mind? Are you doing the things that you think need to be done, and how do you feel about yourself in the process? Sometimes people who are really organic and busy recycling and being green can get really righteous. That's kind of awkward. You're like, "I'm the best because I'm the greenest." Okay. So, is being the best the goal? Or is managing the resources the goal? Because apparently being the best seems to be the most important thing to you and you've just decided being green is the way to be best instead of being a CEO and being the best.

That's a really interesting exploration for us. If you're worried about overpopulation and you're worried about resource management, of course, first start with yourself and then see if you're getting too righteous about the whole thing or too rigid. It's all here for you to learn about you. That's the bottom line. That's why it was given to you, so you could learn about you.

Crisis

We learn by crisis. Does it appear that we're getting it or do we need bigger and bigger crisis's to move ahead?

That's actually a very interesting question because it is true that humans, in general, tend to learn through crisis and tend to learn through deadlines. So it's accurate to say, "We tend to learn through crisis." And it's also something we try to help you guys change. We work on that a lot so that your triggers become red flags alerting you to something to consider working with instead of having to become a 2x4-upside-the-head type crisis.

Do crises need to escalate in order for people to learn? For some people, yes. That's probably always going to be true that some people only learn from crises. Does it have to be true for you? No. Will you observe it in your world even when it stops being true for you? Maybe. Probably. It's a very strong cultural dynamic.

There are cultural dynamics you're not going to be able to do a damn thing about. It's your relationship to the cultural dynamics—just like we talked about overpopulation or being green—these are cultural dynamics that you determine your relationship to. You don't have to live out certain cultural dynamics, but you need to determine your relationship to them because they're not necessarily going to go away because some people are still learning from them. Some people are still playing in that sandbox and if enough people are playing in that sandbox then it's prevalent. It doesn't have to be your way of learning; you don't have to lump yourself in with everybody. That's the beauty about living consciously; you look at each thing and you determine your relationship to it. Your relationship to the stuff that's happening is up to you.

Comment: As a follow up, when I first joined the group, we used to talk about reaching a tipping point. It would be interesting for a compare you to you, Eloheim follow-up.

You're starting to more and more frequently have experiences where you're living from a conscious perspective first. You don't have to have a trigger and then say, "Oh yeah, wait a second, how do I react to that trigger?" You have a trigger and you immediately know, "Oh here it is. I need to be more conscious. I need to look at it again. It's bringing up my core emotion. It's bringing up static. It's bringing up baggage. It's giving me an opportunity to have a choice point." You are choosing your reaction to your creation. We really feel like you guys have come to a tipping point, especially the people we talk to on a regular basis; there's been a big change. There's been a huge change, actually. And again, that's why we have the tool compare you to you because if you don't compare you to you, you may never feel the change. There's always something more that you're struggling with, there's always another thing that you're growing from, there's always another issue that you want to be able to handle more consciously. Your invitation is to recognize that you have changed and as you recognize that you have changed to use that to encourage yourself to keep at it.

Someone said to us recently, "Sometimes I just think it's not really working or nothing's really happening." This is interesting to us because sometimes when you have thoughts like that, it's actually proof that things are changing because you want more change. You've had some change and you want more change. Maybe it's not coming as fast as you'd like, but that doesn't mean you haven't made progress.

Safe areas

Regarding 2012, are there any safe areas?

The safe area is always inside of you. This is part of what we're really helping people with is recognizing that you carry your safety with you wherever you go. A way to visualize this is: A tornado goes through a neighborhood. One house is left standing. Was 432 Main Street the safe area? Those people likely didn't feel very safe with the tornado screaming through their yard, but their house happened to be intact afterward. Now, someone whose house is not intact and someone whose house is intact may have completely different relationships to the experience. The person whose house is intact may feel worse with survivors guilt and, "Oh God, is it safe to live here because look, nobody else was safe." The person whose house is gone may say, "This is horrific, but we needed a change. I was always worried I would have a tornado in my yard living here."

The one thing we would like to make clear is this: You are each having unique individual experiences. You could move to a "safe" place and fall down and break your leg walking across your front yard. Then you might say, "It wasn't safe because I broke my leg here." Or you could stay where you are and an earthquake or a tsunami or a volcano could happen and your house could wash away and your family could end up being closer than it's ever been before and you could say, "I actually feel safer because that happened to me." We can't tell you what will make you feel safe. All we can do is give you tool after tool after tool to help you discover what your relationship to safety is.

Corruption

If it's true that everyone is going to ascend anyway, what's the point in all the work that we're doing? The usual answer is to pave the way for others, which sounds like service mentality, which I know you're not a fan of. Why are we doing this? So all the corrupt bankers can ascend?

This is a question that actually has been running around the light worker community for a couple of decades or more. If two decades ago you were waiting on the 100th monkey thing and living in suffering and victimhood, you passed up two decades of possibility of living in bliss all because you didn't want to help corrupt bankers ascend.

Let that sink in.

It's not present in your external world unless it's true in your internal world. If the corrupt bankers get under your skin, you need to look at what your relationship to corruption is and how corruption is part of everyone's life. Everyone has corruption in their life. If this is your trigger, then there's something about corruption that you need to explore.

Is the 100th monkey thing true? The 100th monkey thing has

some validity in that the more people on the planet that are vibrating at a high rate and living consciously and offering that as an energetic possibility simply by breathing, the more likely other people who never knew about that option will learn about it and choose it as a path.

HERE'S AN EXAMPLE: Let's say you have a whole bunch of people running around getting sunburn on their faces and some people start wearing hats to prevent sunburn. The sunburned people look at the hat people and say, "Oh you mean if you wear a hat you don't get a bad sunburn? I think I'll wear a hat, too." Does that mean that the hat-wearers shouldn't have bothered to wear the hat because it helped a lot of other people not get a sunburn? Of course not.

Would you rather the corrupt banker sit and stew in his corruption or would you rather him transform? Not that he's your business anyway, but just taking that question to its logical conclusion: Is because he's a corrupt banker he doesn't deserve to ascend? Because there are corrupt bankers, are you going to put your growth on hold?

Every single one of you has things you're ashamed of, which we refer to as shadow places. We know it. We can see it in your energy field. Ask yourself, "What is it that I'm ashamed of and how can I transform my relationship to that shame?" Then, when you see a corrupt banker you can have fascination about the banker's decision about how to live and maybe some compassion about "Wow, a lot of people don't like you and that must be uncomfortable energetically and thanks, you showed me a path I don't want to take. You showed me a path I don't want to take. Thank you. And since all experiences are going to be experienced, I'm glad you're experiencing having a bunch of people thinking you're evil instead of me having to experience a bunch of people thinking I'm evil. I've got enough little bits in me that I think are evil and it would be really hard if everyone knew about them."

You all have things about yourself that you don't like; if the corrupt bankers put a face on it then, "Thanks, you put a face on something I don't like about me; this will make it easier for me to heal this issue."

Remember, it all comes back to "What's in your lap" and what are you avoiding by looking at someone and going, "Yuck." You've probably heard it before: point one finger toward someone else, look at how many fingers are pointing back at you. Gotta be really careful about that finger-pointing thing.

How to prepare

How can I deal with my fear and anxiety regarding 2012? Is there anything I should do to prepare for it?

This question gives us an opportunity to actually tell you what we think 2012 is.

2012 is a culmination of energy, meaning a lot of people have put a lot of energy on this date. You really respond to formatting time. You really respond to someone saying, "On this day something is going to happen—you'd better be ready." 2012 has become this idea of, "Something could happen, would happen, will happen and how can I relate to it?"

It seems that people are relating to 2012 primarily from fear. We invite you to have a different relationship to it. Let's have a relationship to it as the coming of a point of focus, of an opportunity to really say, "Why am I afraid of it? What is in my lap that I don't want to look at? Why am I listening to people saying that it's going to be a disaster more than listening to people who say it's going to just be an opportunity for personal growth? Why am I choosing the focus I'm choosing?"

Here is another way to look at it, pick any other "special" date, as an example, the Fourth of July. You may have different options for how you will spend the day. You realize, "I need to decide if I should go to the parade or go to the boating party. I could go to either one and I have to choose."

Exactly! You get to choose. Just like you get to choose your relationship to the "special" date of 2012. Just like a holiday, there's a lot of cultural attention placed there, which gives you an opportunity. It's as if you're in the ocean and a wave is rising up underneath you. Are you going to surfboard it, are you going to try to body surf it, are you just going to enjoy going up and down? What are you going to do? You get to choose. It's an opportunity.

The energy of 2012 can be worked with today. You don't have to wait. Just say to that energy, that rising of attention, that feeling of a focal point of desire for change, "I'm not going to wait until December of 2012. I'm going to have it be now. I'm going to be that way now. That way of 'I wish to focus more consistently on my inner transformation and on my relationship to safety and fears.'"

What will happen after 2012?

More of the same but it's likely a lot more people will be desiring the consciousness path or the personal-growth path. They will have had to look at their fears in a new way and so it may be that more people are fascinated by their internal journey than were before 2012. That's the outcome we'd like to see happen because we think it would be a really interesting exploration. But it's going to be 2013 and just like every other change of year, everybody's going to say, "Oh, I have to write 2013 on my checks now." But we also feel that the people who have really worked consciously and have really studied and have really wanted to grow will feel different in 2013 because you will feel like you've gone past an important point where things did shift for you. It doesn't mean the Earth shifted or the aliens came, it just means that you made your own personal transformation.

2012 is close and so the opportunity is here to use all that bustle that's been created around it and generate an opportunity for you to use that for your own exploration of yourself. When 2013 comes and you can say, "Okay, now I'm taking a new version of me into the world." That's really what we see happening. You guys are growing and then you get to take a new version of you into the world and have experiences that will be colored or seen or experienced by that new version of you. You have a new version of you every moment but we feel like with the up-swell of energetic focus that 2012 happens to be that it will give you the opportunity to have that in a more profound way. It's the same in a smaller magnitude as when you have 11/11/11 or 10/10/10. Everyone says, "It's 10/10/10, let's have a celebration!" But on 10/11/10, you're still you. Maybe you had something profound happen on 10/10/10, but you're still you. Maybe you're a little different—most likely—because every moment, you're changing.

Use the energy of 2012 to facilitate your personal growth. Whether it be dealing with fears and anxieties or allowing yourself to make your own personal goal. "Between now and December 2012 I'm going to really focus on living consciously." You can use it in that way. That's a great way. How do you focus on living consciously? Know why you do what you do. When you get triggered, when you're in fear, when you're confused about uncertainty, choose a different way of responding. The primary way to say it is this: have different relationships to habits. We're happy to help you make that shift. Our books, audio recordings, and video replays are all focused on this.

To sum up, the idea here is that you're here to grow. You're here to transform. You're here to have a different relationship to your habits. You're here to have a different relationship to being human. And everything is being done from the non-physical realms to support that and nothing's being done to detract from that. Sometimes those that are non-physical get this rap like we are making your life hard or holding out on you—there's this sense of, "God, you guys know everything and you don't tell us or the aliens or the this or that's are going to come and make it hard on us." Actually, that couldn't be further from the truth. The truth is everything is being done to give you the growth opportunities that you desired when you came here in the first place.

This entire place, this entire solar system, this beautiful planet, these amazing bodies, all of it has been crafted very carefully to give you this opportunity. That's the gift, and how you interact with it that gift is your privilege. Your free will gives you the option to not care one little bit about it or you can think it's the most precious thing or you can be right in the middle. It doesn't matter. It's free will. It's the greatest thing. You guys are having this extraordinary experience.

Tools

Point fingers

You can't point fingers anymore, meaning you no longer have the option of saying that someone else or something else creates in your life. Nothing else can create in your life, and every time you point your finger and decide how it's going to be, and decide and decide and decide, you're turning over the only power you have in this life, which is the power to create your reality using your free will. You can go right along living the victim mentality quite nicely, but if you actually want to experience the magnificence that's possible with the Homo sapiens moving into Homo spiritus paradigm you have to stop looking at other people and other things as creating in your reality and start to recognize and acknowledge that you are the one. You are the one who put it there.

It can be hard when you realize, "Oh my God, I point fingers every second of every day." However, this realization allows you to access the wow of responsibility, the wow of creatorship, the wow of: "Yes, I did that. Yes, I did that. I did it for me. I did it for me so that I could have the experience that that scenario offers me."

The idea that you can't point fingers at anybody anymore is a radical concept. It says, "Everybody in my life, everything in my life, is my creation. And as my creation I take 100 percent responsibility for it being there and I take 100 percent responsibility for how I choose to interact with it." When you stop pointing fingers, it's not: "Why the hell is this in my life?" It's: "Wow, this is in my life!" And that's a big shift. That's a big shift. It was a big shift to get into 100 percent responsibility, even if taking 100 percent responsibility meant "I'm taking responsibility even though I don't like it." Now it's: "I'm taking responsibility, I know there's something here for me, I don't have to figure it out as much as I have to allow myself to experience it without throwing barrier after barrier after barrier up between me and the experience."

***

Veronica writes:

I remember quite clearly the night that The Council talked with us about no more pointing fingers. I was struck with the power of this idea. It really is quite a shift to go from seeing yourself as a victim to realizing you are a creator. Then, to start realizing that you created everything (even the shitty bits!), well, that's a doozy. To further realize that you can't pin it on anyone else, even when they "did" it… it's a lot of responsibility. However, it's my responsibility to work with my creations and my reactions to them. This puts the ball in my court, which suits me just fine.

***

The part I remember about "pointing fingers" is that when I point my finger at someone else, one finger is pointing away from me and the other three fingers are pointing back at me. Just a little reminder that I created this situation to show me something about myself. I created it to have a learning experience, which is liberat-

ing. *Taking responsibility for my creations instead of spinning and suffering in victimhood is quite a relief.*

—*Mary T*

***

It is really easy to point fingers at any person and say "This is happening because you did this." That is pointing fingers at someone else instead of saying that I have created this to learn from it. I am taking the power of creating what happens to (for) me instead of simply going along for the ride. It gives a person a sense of confidence that you have a hand in what is going on.

—*Rosie*

What's in your lap?

When you are tempted to get into somebody else's business or find yourself judging people and/or events, ask yourself "What's in my lap? What is going on in me? How does this reflect something in me?" You can't tell anybody else what they need to see or what they are seeing; you need to deal with what's in your lap.

Are you in this moment? What static are you aware of? Where are you lying to yourself? What are you afraid of?

Need we go on? There is PLENTY for you to focus on right there in your lap.

***

Veronica writes:

I love this, "Need we go on?" Eloheim specifically told me to put that in there.

***

I use this tool a lot when I'm triggered by my birth family. We have a lot of issues around lack that we've been working out with each other from the time we were children. So now, when one of my siblings calls to complain about not having enough money, I look at what it brings up in me, what's in my lap, and it helps me to not go into "savior" mode. When I am conscious about this, it amazes me how much the conversation can change.

—Claire

What is true now?

Asking yourself "What is true now?" is a way of staying connected to the moment and your soul's insight about the moment.

It's fairly easy to remember to say "What is true now," but it's also very easy to be habitual about the answer you allow yourself to experience. What is true now is not answered by the mind. What is true now is answered by an "aha" from the soul, so by asking yourself what is true now constantly, you're creating a very strong connection between you and your soul, which is a fine thing to do if you're interested in transforming your life. The truth of you must be experienced consciously.

If what is true now is answered by a sentence of, say, more than say 10 words, it's your mind. An "aha" from the soul is going to be shorter than that. It doesn't need to be lengthy because it's not processed by the mind. It's an energetic truth expressed briefly in order to really sink in. If what is true now starts to have a lengthy explanation, suspect that the mind is encroaching on the soul's turf and ask the mind to shut up.

When used with consistency and consciousness, what is true now can be used to uncover unconscious coping mechanisms and lies that you tell yourself.

Veronica writes:

Another tool to keep very close to you. I use this one a lot to help sort out when I am acting from my current preferences and when I am acting habitually or out of patterns from the past.

***

I like "what is true now." I find the greatest challenge is being aware when the chatter-y monkey-mind starts with its unsuspectingly clever maneuvering to make me feel uncomfortable or irritated or going around and around on the same conversation. Old news, stuff that is past its expiry date, as they say. When I realize it, I immediately go to "what is true now." What is usually "true now" is that I was enjoying whatever I was doing before the sneaky bits got into my conscious thoughts. It seems never-ending.

—*Rosie*

You to you (compare)

Stop and pat yourself on the back every once in a while, won't you? Your inner truth is externalized through your life, and a lot of times it's the crappy bits that you notice. But we want you to start paying attention to the bits that reflect an internal journey that's actually moving toward bliss, that's actually on a transformational path. Because that's the truth of it. The truth of it is that you're on a transformational path and things are changing and it's easy to get lost in the changes if they're challenging. But the truth is, comparing you to you, you are transforming. And you need to be patting yourself on the back, giving yourself credit, and mentioning to your friends the things that are transforming in you in order to give them the kind of publicity within you that the shitty bits get. Publicize your transformation. Or at least notice it, at a minimum.

You are constantly in a pattern of transformation. If you don't do compare you to you, you're likely to feel like you are in one never-ending problem. When you compare you to you, you stop for a moment to realize, "Well, this is a different thing I'm dealing with now. That other issue shifted, so maybe I can try those tools with this new trigger."

Veronica writes:

This tool has such a loving feeling to it. You are making progress. You are transforming. You are changing. It is happening. Stop and allow yourself to see it. Love yourself for the progress you have made. Be fascinated by the journey yet to come.

***

I'm so focused on moving forward all the time, I sometimes forget to do this. But when I remember this tool, I love myself for who I am—again.

—*Randy Sue Collins*

***

Compare you to you allows me to step out of an old situation and instantly reevaluate it with a fresh outlook.

—*Mike*

***

Comparing me to me in stressful situations has been both fascinating and encouraging. There is always a gem of progress to be seen and felt that keeps my heart light and gives me courage to keep on keeping on.

—*Deb*

***

I find this tool extremely helpful in measuring my progress over time. How would a similar issue have affected me in the past? "Compare you to you" is a perfect measuring stick for gauging personal growth.

—*Murster*

***

Compare U2U is such an affirming tool. It is so great to feel the progress I'm making. It is so sweet and so fair to leave everyone else out of the picture and just relish how far I've come. Nothing inspires like success, right?

—*Anna R., Mexico*

Terms

These terms were defined by Eloheim and the Council, mostly in a group setting.

2012

The year 2012 is a shifting point on your calendar; a place of attention in order to help you focus. This is not a deadline, but a focal point to help facilitate your desire for consciousness and your desire for transformation. It is not a fixed point in time. The "place" of 2012 is a potential for dramatic transformation. That "place" is meeting you where you are; from there you create the transformation that you desire both as a human and as a soul.

5D

Shorthand term for the soul expressing the human form with a consciousness-based operating system. 5D is the experience of Homo spiritus, where the body is lived from an ensouled perspective.

Aha

A moment of clarity and insight that comes from accessing the soul's perspective; contrast this with the repetitive hamster-wheel-mind habit of thinking.

Ahas are commonly experienced while in the shower or doing other tasks that don't require full attention. The path of ascension and the choice for consciousness facilitate experiencing a steady stream of ahas.

Akashic Record

The galactic Internet.

A term that reflects the totality of: all of the lifetimes of those who have experienced Earth, all of the time that one has spent between lifetimes, all of the time spent in other incarnational opportunities, and all the time spent as a soul doing whatever the soul wanted to do. Think of a giant library where you each have your own section or file containing everything that has ever been recorded regarding what you've done, how you've lived, and what you've encountered. This isn't kept in anything that would resemble a library but it is helpful to think of it in this way conceptually.

Your Akashic Record is a reservoir of information that makes up the body of your soul. The energy that reflects that reservoir of information is what would be correlated to the physicality of the soul, if the soul had physicality.

When you are not in body and encounter another soul, your section of the Akashic Records is the information presented to the other soul. Your Akashic Record is the information that your soul presents to other souls at first glance.

Alternate expressions

Your "past and future" lives. Since time is not linear, these so-called "past and future" lives are all happening simultaneously; therefore your "other" lives can be referred to as alternate expressions of you.

Amnesia

The term we use to describe the "clean slate" of forgetfulness that a human experiences to facilitate living in physical form. It is a necessary state of being to incarnate into the physical body. Amnesia allows you to focus on the present moment in the present lifetime, without distractions from other lifetimes.

If you did not have amnesia about previous Earth experiences and incarnations it would be virtually impossible to stay in the moment because you'd be too busy wanting to go finish, redo, or undo things that have happened in alternate expressions.

Ascension

Ascension is a gradual, albeit drastic, transformation from a fear-based operating system into a consciousness-based operating system. Ascension requires evolution in the physical form and a radical shift in the way you respond to the biological messages the body offers.

Ascension is the term assigned to the energetic of the evolutionary leap into Homo spiritus. The Homo spiritus energetic allows for a life to be lived from the soul's perspective, and for a transformed way of interacting with physical matter.

Ascension does not mean you're leaving the body or the planet. Ascension means you're experiencing being in-body on Earth in a brand-new way that is a higher-vibrational, conscious way of living from your soul's perspective in which a spiritual partnership is formed between the soul, physical form, and personality self.

Baggage

The past, future, cultural pressures, DNA pressures, habits, triggers, and other static that get in the way of you experiencing the moment.

Bliss

The state of living in a spiritual partnership with your soul as a high-vibrational, conscious being. The state resulting from having tools for conscious living, being in neutral observation, and knowing that an experience previously judged as wrong (or right) is actually an opportunity for learning and growth. Living in a state of bliss is the result of living in the consciousness-based operating system, as Homo spiritus.

Boundaries

Using your ability as a creator while living in a free-will zone to choose what you are interested in experiencing; directing the incarnation.

Certainty

When you are operating from the fear-based operating system, change feels extremely risky. The survival instinct is constantly pressuring you to stay the same, because "the same" has kept you alive. Any changes to "the same" require certainty about the outcome in order to quiet the fears the survival instinct produces. As certainty is a fallacy—you can't be truly certain of anything in the diverse, vast world you find yourself in—you find yourself in a no-win situation: Change requires certainty, certainty is unattainable, and paralysis (fear) is the result.

Evolving your relationship to the survival instinct and certainty is a major aspect of the ascension process.

Chakra

Energy centers in the body. Traditionally, there are seven major chakras: Root (1st), Sexuality (2nd), Power (3rd), Heart (4th), Throat (5th), Third eye (6th), and Crown (7th). We use the idea of chakras as a handy reference tool. It's a shortcut that allows us to talk about different aspects of your body and energetic system without having to go into a long explanation each time. It is not required that you believe in chakras to follow the conversation.

Change

The recognition of an altered condition in the incarnation, which, if processed habitually, often triggers fear. When processed consciously, change becomes the mechanism for growth.

Channel

An incarnated soul experiencing the human form that allows non-physical guides to communicate through him or her in order to present helpful information in a palatable form. If out-of-body or non-corporal guides showed up as a burning bush, beam of light, or in a light body of some fashion, they would be far more likely to create fear than comfort. Channeling and channels allow a more human-to-human type of transmission of information, commonly less triggering than other types of transmissions.

Choose your reactions to your creations

"I am 100 percent responsible for my reactions to my creations." That's one of the most conscious things you can say. We strongly recommend that you write that down and stick it on your bathroom mirror.

"I am a creator; I created it all. It's all here for me, and, I choose how I react to my creations as well." When something occurs, don't look for it to be different. Don't say, "I wish it were some other way." Say, "What is here right now is here on purpose. It's here because it needs to be here to facilitate my growth." Then, take it further; take your acknowledgment of the truth of you as a creator to the point where you can also say, "I am choosing the reaction I have to every single experience in my life. All of it."

It is your responsibility to set boundaries, state preferences, tell the truth about your creations, and to make sure that your creations bring out the authenticity of you, which you can then share. That's the gift of creating and choosing your reactions to your creations, it lets you share the truth of you. Consistently emanate the truth of you regardless of the circumstances you find yourself in by choosing your reactions based on your high-vibrational, conscious experiences of yourself.

Conscious/Consciousness

Knowing why you do what you do. Choosing your reactions. Not being driven by habit. Experiencing the world as a creator rather than as a victim.

The world, as you experience it, has been programmed through habits, fears, and your biology. Through attention (consciousness), you can live the bigger picture that includes your personality's paradigm shifting and the embracing of your soul's perspective, as well.

Consciousness-based operating system (CBOS)

The consciousness-based operating system is the 5-D or Homo spiritus way of experiencing the world that allows for conscious interactions with experiences rather than fear-based, habitually driven interaction with experiences.

Core Emotion (CE)

Your core emotion is a theme present in every thought, action, feeling, dream, hope, experience, and desire. It is present in all moments of your life. Your core emotion is unique to you and unique to this lifetime. Discovering your core emotion often answers long-standing questions such as: "Why does this keep happening?" "Why do all my relationships follow the same pattern?" "Why can't I get past this blockage in my path?"

Most people experience their core emotion from an unconscious or unhealed perspective. Learning to work with your core emotion from a healed or conscious perspective is often described as "life-changing." Since the core emotion is present in all aspects of your life, bringing consciousness to the core emotion brings consciousness to all aspects of your life.

NOTE: The exploration of your core emotion is one of our specialties. We have a specific process for revealing your core emotion and helping you move from an unhealed to a healed relationship with it. Because of the intensely personal nature of this exploration and the time required to fully explore it, we only offer this process through private sessions. For more information, see the contact page.

Creating your reality

"Create your own reality" is one of those terms that's overused and under-understood. Creating your reality is often believed to be a way to control your reality. It is thought to be a path to certainty and safety. Creating your reality is actually an outcome of your vibrational self, your vibrational nature, your emanation of a higher-vibrational choice.

Creating your reality works very much like a fountain. The fountain shoots up the water and it sprays out all over the place. No one knows where every drop's going to land. Who would want to? It would be tedious in the extreme. The uncertainty creates the beauty.

Similarly, creating your reality isn't about the outcome (where the drops land), it is about the experience (the beauty of the water in the air.)

In our fountain example, the water represents the truth of you (your soul's perspective and your personality), the water pressure represents your free-will choices and the fountain mechanism represents your preferences and boundaries.

Creating your reality starts with setting boundaries in association with your preferences, you then align your free-will to choose conscious reactions to your experiences (which often has the result of clearing static), and then you and your soul emanate together.

You initiate your creation, you choose how you react to your creation, and you remain open to insight from your soul.

Creator, The

If you believe that this world is created, then there must be a Creator. Therefore, the Creator is the one who created all. It helps to recognize that the Creator is not conceivable in its entirety while experiencing duality because of the inherent limitations of the human mind and the infinite scope of the Creator. However, the Creator can be sensed through insight from your soul and through experiencing creation.

Creator/creatorship

The acknowledgement that you are in a free-will zone and that you have the ability to choose your reactions to your experiences. When creations seem to be in opposition to what we "want," creators recognize that there are levels of creation and that everything is happening *for* me, rather than falling into victimhood.

Cultural pressures

Cultural pressures include: family beliefs, societal norms, and customs. Often cultural pressures present as, "It's what everyone else is doing" and are used to justify forgoing transformation.

Habits and DNA pressures combine with cultural pressures to make a potent combination for habitual response to triggers.

Density

Experiencing the free-will zone in a body. Souls do not have physical form in the same way humans do. Incarnating on Earth provides for the unique experience of density, duality, and free will.

DNA pressures

Your DNA is the blueprint for your body. You and your soul collaborated to create the unique incarnation you are experiencing.

We use the term "DNA pressures" to refer to the interaction habits and consciousness have with your physicality.

As an example: Tall people put things on high shelves while shorter people will habitually put things on lower shelves. Both are examples of people acting based on DNA (and convenience).

DNA pressures combine with cultural pressures to make a potent combination for habitual response to triggers.

Duality

The idea that there are only two options, typically experienced as either, "what I think is right and what I think is wrong," or "what they think is right and what they think is wrong." A very limited way to experience Earth and the human form. The fear-based operating system loves duality because it gives a false sense of certainty. (I am RIGHT). The consciousness-based operating system leaves duality behind as it explores the truth of, "Everything that happens, happens for me and is teaching me something."

Earth

The planet Earth is designated as a free-will zone and was developed to provide opportunities for incarnating souls to experience density and duality. Earth, at this time, is engaged in an ascension process and will reflect a changed environment for ascended beings to explore. What that changed environment will actually look like is unknown, and highly anticipated for that very reason.

Eloheim

We, the Eloheim, are a collaboration of souls presenting with a singular voice, channeled through the body of Veronica Torres with her explicit approval, willingness, and allowance. It is our great privilege to offer our support to you at this very exciting time on Earth to facilitate the transformation of Homo sapiens to Homo spiritus; moving from the fear-based operating system to the consciousness-based operating system. It is a grand experiment that many beings in the universe are watching with great interest, awe, and fascination.

Emanating (the truth of you)

As you live consciously, you emanate consciousness into your world. Your job is just to contribute, your job is not to try to dictate or control where your contribution to high-vibrational living ends up. It's not your business where it goes or how it shows up in the world.

Energetics

The way that souls communicate through nonverbal knowing. Because your physical forms cannot yet communicate on the level that souls do, nonverbal knowing or "energetics" need to be translated into your language to facilitate understanding and communication.

Since it is always less accurate to use language than it is to communicate energetically, it is our hope and desire that your progress will eventually include the ability to communicate energetically without the need for language.

Energetic communication is happening all the time. Living consciously means that you are emanating a conscious energetic. It really does matter how you handle triggers and other upsets. Not just because it determines how you will experience the triggers, but it also determines how your emanation will go out to others. When we work with you, we are reading your energetics far more than we are listening to your words. Your energetics often show us visuals, which we can use to facilitate deeper understanding of the situations you are experiencing.

Ensoulment

The process by which soul energy is more deeply experienced by the personality incarnated in the physical form as the perspective is shifted from one of a survival instinct to a soul's perspective—from a fear-based operating system to a consciousness-based operating system.

Ensoulment, or living from the soul's perspective, is a collaboration between the personality self (you incarnate as a human) and your soul's wisdom. Don't misunderstand this to be that your soul "takes you over." This is not the case.

As an example, let's say you take a calculus class. The you at the end of the class hasn't 'taken over' the you from the beginning of the class. You have become a being that has the additional experience of the wisdom you gained in your studies.

Ensoulment is you realizing the wisdom and insight your soul already has; the completeness of you.

Fear

Fear is a biological reaction to change or the idea of change that typically creates the "fight or flight" response in the body, which is an adrenaline-based response to, "What do I do next?" Typically, the answer is that you run habit.

Consciously experiencing fear presents opportunities for extreme growth because it gives you the opportunity to break habitual patterns—to experience the moment rather than experiencing habit, which often involves projection of the future or bringing a memory of the past into the moment.

Fear can also be defined as the biological component of duality. It is the biological response to the belief in duality that is enacted regardless of which side of duality you're on. If you're on the side of duality that says, "This is wrong," then there's fear for survival. If you're on the side that says, "This is right," there's fear that it won't continue.

Fear and the survival instinct work together to keep you small.

Fear-based

Actions based on fear rather than conscious choice. A habitual, unconscious mentality (operating system) based on fear.

Fear-based operating system (FBOS)

You are a fear-based being. It is not something you can argue with. It is a fact. Period. Full stop. End of sentence. You cannot argue with the fact that you are a fear-based being because you have been built to operate from fear in order to continue surviving. You've been built to startle at loud noises. You've been built to have the fight-or-flight response trigger in you. You've been built to be wary and aware of your surroundings. All of this can be summarized or reduced to fear. There is no need to be ashamed of admitting the fears that you find yourself experiencing because it is a core aspect of being human. You were brought into this incarnation running the fear-based operating system, meaning you're constantly experiencing the world based on fear. The survival instinct is continuously asking you to be wary. The survival instinct is continuously trying to keep you small and it has extreme measures it can go to in order to keep you from sticking your neck out, from standing out in the crowd, from being noticed. The survival instinct flares up in you and requires your habitual responses to stimulus and triggers.

As consciousness is applied to the fear-based operating system, and as you break out of habitual response patterns, you're able to experience what is going on in your life from a new perspective and shift into a consciousness-based operating system.

Free will

Free will is the opportunity to be in amnesia about the truth of you, the truth of your infinite, immortal nature.

Free will allows you to experience Earth as YOU see fit. No one can interfere with your chosen experience—not your soul, and not even The Creator.

Note, we said your chosen experience. You choose how you experience everything. Your free will gives you this ability. Now, we are not saying that everything that happens in your life feels like something you have chosen on a personality level; however, your chosen reaction to everything that happens in your life is within your purview.

Free will gives you the option to break out of the fear-based operating system, to break habits, exercise change and choose consciousness.

Free-will zone

An experiment that was initiated by The Eloheim after being invited by The Creator to come up with something new for souls to experience. It is an opportunity for souls to incarnate in a completely amnesic state and live a lifetime through their own direction, without influence from external forces, to grow as a soul. The free-will zone is inclusive of the solar system that holds Earth.

Growth

Consciousness infusing the incarnation resulting in transformation.

Guides

A generic or general term used for beings that are not currently in physical form that are available to assist those who are in physical form, through a variety of means—through channels through coincidence, through synchronicities, through dreams, and many other ways.

Habit/Habitual response

Habit is tied into the fear of getting dead and the survival instinct. Since the body is programmed to stay alive, it will say, "Well, this hasn't killed me yet, so let's continue." Change makes the body feel like there's a potential to get killed. Change means new factors to manage, new things to deal with, and new situations to juggle. It is easier on the body if it already knows the threats that are involved in your day-to-day life and has already established that none of them are threatening enough to get you dead. The body is going to want to keep repeating that pattern. If you know that a food is poisonous to you, you don't eat it again—making that a healthy habit. But the survival instinct, as translated into 21st-century Earth, ends up looking like, "I can't quit this job that I hate because I'm too afraid of getting dead. I'm too engrained in this habit to try something else."

Hamster-wheel thinking

The habitual mind repetitiously trying to think its way out of "problems." Repetitious thinking about past and/or future experiences misses the experience of the moment.

High-vibrational

High-vibrational refers to actions, thoughts, ideas, and relationships which are based on consciousness and conscious choices. It is not a judgmental term; rather it is descriptive of the fact that your body is actually vibrating at a different rate than it did before you infused consciousness into your life.

Your soul vibrates at a very high rate. Raising your vibration by living consciously is a very important step in living from your soul's perspective and walking the path of ascension.

Homo spiritus

A name for a state of being that is possible when you live in collaboration with your soul incorporating your soul's perspective; a transformed, expanded experience of the physical form and a shifted paradigm of how one is on Earth.

Living from the consciousness-based operating system, pursuing the path of ascension.

Insight

Information received directly from your soul.

The challenge when explaining the word "insight" is that it is a process that uses the brain but must not be confused with "thinking."

There are a few characteristics that illuminate the differences between the two: the mind is limited and will often present limiting messages. The mind's messages are repetitive and often negative. Insight will present ideas and options you've never considered before, which are always positive and constructive in their nature. Insight will never demean you; it will never be negative and it will always be supportive of your growth and transformation.

Light worker

A soul incarnating at this time with the specific desire to grow spiritually and live consciously. A person walking the path of ascension. A Homo sapiens desiring to live as Homo spiritus.

Learning

As an incarnate soul, the processes that you go through in order to have the growth you desire is called "learning." The journey is a journey of change, shifts, transformation, and ascension, which is all brought into the physical system through the process of internal and external transformation, a reflection of all of the learning that has occurred.

Mind

The mind's thoughts and insight are both processed by the brain. The mind is only capable of taking the spiritual journey so far. At some point, the mind's ability to manage the spiritual journey comes to a standstill. Without the infusion of insight from the soul, the journey will stagnate. When you act, react, and create only from your mind, you're cutting yourself off from the vast resources of your soul and the Akashic Records. In this context it's easy to see that allowing the mind to run the incarnation is limiting.

Personality

The aspect of the incarnate human that has a name, that has preferences, that has a history, that has a future, that has relationships. It's the aspect of you that's currently under development.

The power of the personality is that it wields free will. Therefore, the personality actually is completely in charge of the incarnation by controlling whether or not consciousness is employed, deciding how to react to situations, and deciding whether or not to pursue ascension.

Safety

The idea that you can control outcomes. Safety is sought by looking for certainty. Certainty is a fallacy—it can never be achieved. Everything has some degree of uncertainty in it. The survival instinct constantly pushes you to seek safety; the fear-based operating system gives you no way to get there. The asecension journey helps you learn that the only sense of true safety comes from a deep connection to your soul and moving moment to moment through clarity.

Shadow

The aspects of yourself that you don't want anybody else to know about; the things that you are ashamed of and deny, and repress; places where you don't love yourself yet, parts of you that you reject as unacceptable, wrong, bad, or even evil; aspects of your life you feel are socially unacceptable yet still true; honest experiences that you have had that you didn't handle with consciousness; shame: these form your shadow.

We see your shadow aspects as dark holes or gray areas in your energy body that make you look a bit like Swiss cheese.

Our desire is to help you love all parts of yourself, which allows you to live from the soul's perspective as a Homo spiritus being.

Soul

The infinite, immortal nature of your true self, including the collection of every lifetime you've had on Earth, the time between lifetimes, every lifetime you've had in other incarnational opportunities, and all other experiences.

The soul is a vast reservoir of experience and an eternally curious being.

Animating a human body does not require the entirety of your soul. There is no way you can stuff an entire soul into a human body. But there's a percentage of your soul that has been allocated to be experience-able in this lifetime.

Soul's perspective

The wisdom of your soul incorporated into your experience of being human. It's the insight available to you when you live from the consciousness-based operating system.

From the soul's perspective, there is no judgment, no duality, no fear about life in the physical form. Everything is fascinating.

Your soul knows this is all just a journey in learning. There's no right, there's no wrong, there's no good, there's no bad. It's a journey in learning, exploration, experience. It's not the destination—it's the journey.

Spiritual

Functioning from more than just the survival instinct. Awareness of and openness to experiences outside of those that are "provable" or "repeatable." Knowledge that you are more than just this human form.

Static

Unconscious reactions and thoughts; coping mechanisms, masks, lies, baggage, dishonesty, hiding from your authentic expression or the completeness of you, anything that interrupts your ability to stay in the authentic truth of the moment. The mind, the survival instinct, the body, and fear all generate static to keep you small.

Static includes all the reasons you have sold yourself on which you use to avoid presenting the truth of you to the world. It will crop up more intensely as you start to recognize the greatness and the vastness of your true self.

Living consciously is the path to clearing static.

Suffering

Suffering occurs when you experience the world from a victim mentality—not believing you are a creator and instead living in limitation and habit.

You've all suffered, and you have the choice in the suffering to experience it as learning. No matter what is occurring, there's always that choice. Change happens. What is, is. Let's look at it from a new perspective. Do you want to climb out of this new experience with something learned from it, or do you want to wallow in what happened to you, in victimhood?

Survival Instinct

A body-based dynamic that puts the continuation of life at the top of the list of importance. The survival instinct serves you deeply by continuing life even when physical, mental, or emotional experiences lead you to feeling as though you want your life to end.

There had to be a survival instinct put into the system because duality is so different from your experience of being a soul that it would be very tempting to "drop one toe into this water" and then run away. The body's innate survival instinct keeps you in the incarnation long enough to be able to make conscious choices about the experience.

In order to live a conscious life, one must transform one's relationship to the survival instinct. Consciousness asks you to make steps toward change that the survival instinct will be resistant to embrace because to the body, any change feels like potential death and therefore, should be avoided at all costs.

The survival instinct is one of your greatest treasures as well as one of the most challenging places to transform with consciousness because it's so deeply based in the body, and based in unconscious processing. When you are able to consciously modify the way the survival instinct works in the incarnation, you open yourself up to a deep and profound way of re-experiencing how it is to be human. This is one of the major steps in living as Homo spiritus, as an ascended being.

Thinking

The process by which the brain exerts control over the incarnation.

The survival instinct is often the driving force behind thinking.

Thinking is often employed to avoid experiencing change, transformation, or growth. In the spiritual journey, transforming your thought process with consciousness to choose insight from your soul rather than small-mind thinking is one of the major steps to becoming an ascended being.

The brain is the thinking organ. The mind is the thought process. Insight, which comes from your soul, can feel like thinking, however, the content will clarify if you are thinking or receiving insight.

Tools

Techniques used to interrupt the unconscious running of habit by using consciousness to shift out of a fear-based operating system into the consciousness-based operating system. See the table of contents for a list of tools included in this book.

Transformation

A term describing change, especially change along the ascension process.

Triggers

Triggers are stimuli that the personality experiences which bring up opportunities to explore unhealed parts of the personality self.

Unconscious

Acting from the fear-based operating system without the intervention of consciousness; running habit.

Vibration

Low vibration: A state of being that comes from living from the fear-based operating system, not looking for conscious understanding or experience of the dynamics being presented to you. Living habitually rather than opening to new experience.

It is not a judgmental term, rather it is descriptive of the fact that your body is actually vibrating at a different rate than it would if you infused consciousness into your life.

Your soul vibrates at a very high rate. It is difficult to connect to your soul's energy when living a low-vibrational life.

HIGH-VIBRATION: A description of actions, thoughts, ideas, and relationships which are based on consciousness and conscious choices. It is not a judgmental term, rather it is descriptive of the fact that your body is actually vibrating at a different rate than it did before you infused consciousness into your life.

Your soul vibrates at a very high rate. Raising your vibrational by living consciously is a very important step in living from your soul's perspective and walking the path of ascension.

Victim/Victimhood

The mistaken perspective that things happen to you, that you are at the whim of any other creature, being, person, or eventuality that you experience while on Earth. Running the fear-based-operating system. It is a perspective that is very easy to assume because you incarnate with amnesia, making it difficult for you to remember your infinite nature, or the fact that you planned to be here and have the experiences you are having.

When events trigger you or you have experiences that you deem negative, your reaction is, "Why did this happen to me?" which is a victim's perspective. With a conscious journey and a conscious life, you're able to start seeing the world as the creator that you are, and start asking, "Why is this happening for me?" and realizing that "Everything teaches me something."

Your internal world creates your external journey

Your internal world is the creation point for the external expression of your life. Not the other way around. Your internal process is projected on the movie screen of your external life where it all plays out. This allows you to learn and grow from the experience of observing your internal life projected (externalized).

Your internal world is a series of choices that you've made, even if the choice was to default to a habitual pattern, to default to a culturally driven pattern, to default to the childhood pattern. Those are still choices.

Remember, it can't happen in your external world unless it's true in your internal world. When experiences arise, ask, "What are you showing me about me? What are you telling me about me?" Let the experiences inform you rather than staying with the surface reaction of, "They're just triggering me or challenging me or frustrating me or driving me bananas." Ask instead, "What are you showing me about me?"

You can't dictate how people react to you, necessarily, but you can certainly influence the outcome by loving yourself well and sending that into the world instead of doubt and anguish and anxiety and feeling stepped on and being a victim and all that. If you walk into a room knowing you love yourself and emanating your truth, you're going to have a different experience than if you walk into a room feeling like a victim and a doormat. You will be known and reacted to by the way you love yourself.

Your awareness of your internal world becomes so rich and well-developed and well-known and mapped by you that your emanation of the truth of your internal world starts to resemble a fountain that bubbles up and spills over without stopping. It's not something you have to think about or work yourself through or get going. It bubbles up in you and it spills over, just like a fountain does, the fullness of your internal world emanating out into the world. This doesn't involve you acting in the world as much as it involves you experiencing the world from your truth. The truth of you being real.

Who are Eloheim and The Council?

On February 11, 1997, I had a reading by a very skilled psychic and channel. During that reading he said that I would become a channel myself. Although I valued much of what he shared, my reaction to that statement was, YEAH, RIGHT!

I was quite familiar with channeling. I found it incredibly valuable. I just didn't see myself doing it!

That all changed when I came to Sonoma. I was invited to a friend's home to do a Lakshmi puja. The chanting left me in a very altered state. When we finished, we sat in a circle on the floor. I told one of the participants I had a message for her and then shared information she found very helpful. At the end of the sharing I said, "We are the Eloheim and we are pleased to have been with you today."

Now, even though I knew what had happened, I was overwhelmed by it and started to cry. It didn't feel bad or wrong, just very intense. It made me feel very conspicuous. I immediately told myself, "That's never going to happen again."

It was some time before it did. Over time, I got more comfortable with the idea of being a channel but I had no idea how to do it! I tried to work with Eloheim on my own once or twice. I even recorded a very useful message about habitual response on November 26, 2000, yet it just wasn't coming together. Almost two years passed without much forward movement.

Finally, a friend and I figured it out. What was needed was a second person to ask the questions and help me with the logistics of the whole thing.

In the very beginning while channeling, I had to raise my right hand in order to receive the energies (boy, am I glad that I don't have to do that any longer). I would get very thirsty, but I wasn't able to hold a glass (I still have a bunch of straws in a drawer from those days). I had a TON of insecurity about "Am I making this up?" and "Is this real?" and "Am I doing it right?" I needed a lot of reassurance just to stick with it. I would get very sleepy afterward and sometimes needed help just getting around. I had to eat a lot of protein to keep my energy level up.

Details, details, details. All of which felt completely unmanageable to me alone, but became possible once I had help.

After about one month, Eloheim told us that this wasn't just for the two of us and to get a group together. That was September 2002, when we began our weekly Eloheim sessions. We still hold meetings every Wednesday night and one Sunday per month. You can join us live or tune into our webcasts. For more information, please visit: eloheim.com/web-casts.

I had never heard the term Eloheim until they introduced themselves that way. Someone then told me it was one of the names of God. I looked it up on the Internet and found that to be true. It is important to note that although it is common to see the spelling Elohim, I was guided to use the spelling Eloheim.

Eloheim has made it clear that just as not everyone named

John is the same, to not assume that all entities using the name Eloheim or Elohim are the same. The material they present with me is internally consistent and can be taken as a whole.

Eloheim is a group entity that presents with one voice. That one voice feels like a male energy. We refer to the Eloheim as "he" or "they."

They refer to themselves as "we."

Starting on June 10, 2009, I began channeling the rest of The Council. Here are the dates of their first appearances:

The Visionaries - 06/10/2009

The Guardians - 12/02/2009

The Girls - 01/06/2010

The Matriarch - 02/03/2010

The Warrior - 03/17/2010

Fred - 06/30/2010

For more information about Eloheim and The Council, please visit:

eloheim.com/who-is-eloheim

What is channeling?

Channeling is a process where I set my personality aside to allow Eloheim and The Council to use my physical form to convey their teachings.

PLEASE NOTE: This is not possession. It only occurs when I give explicit permission. I can stop it at ANY time.

When I am channeling I feel as though I am standing or sitting behind and to the left of my actual body. I am aware of what is being said as the session unfolds, although I don't always remember everything that is discussed.

Eloheim and The Council specialize in reading the energy of a question, situation, or person. They often experience visual representations of the energy they sense. When this occurs, I see it as a "movie" in my head not unlike what happens when I am dreaming.

I have created a YouTube video with more details about the process. You can watch it by following this link http://youtube.com/EJ2rVvBsB1c.

About the author

Photo credit: nancikerby.com

Veronica Torres: is based in Sonoma, CA. She has channeled Eloheim since 2002, both in public and private sessions. Her public channeling sessions are offered five times a month. These sessions are broadcast live on the Internet and archived for on-demand viewing.

Veronica's career history is interesting and varied, with work including: talk radio host, Rock and Roll memorabilia store owner, Network Director of a Holistic Practitioner's Group, Producer of Well Being Expos, and jewelry designer!

Contact

Website: eloheim.com

Facebook: facebook.com/eloheim

Twitter: twitter.com/channelers

YouTube: youtube.com/eloheimchannel

Join our live channeling sessions in person or online:

eloheim.com/web-casts

Visit our meeting archives for video and audio recordings of past gatherings:

eloheim.com/eloheim-recordings

Join our mailing list:

tinyurl.com/eloheimlist

Private session with Eloheim:

eloheim.com/meeting-schedule-private-sessions/

Preview of other books

Eloheim and The Council books are available online through major book retailers and by visiting http://www.eloheim.com/dlg/cart/index.php.

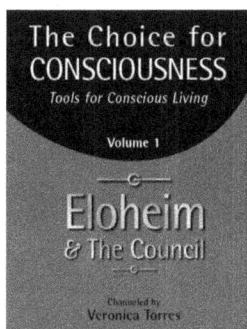

The Choice for Consciousness: Tools for Conscious Living ,
Vol. 1

Why would you want to make the choice for consciousness? What are tools for conscious living?

Two very important questions.

Here are four more: Are you living in peace? Are you living in joy? Are you living in serenity? Are you living in bliss?

And, the most important question: Are you ready to take bold steps in that direction?

Moving out of a fear-based operating system into a consciousness-based operating system allows you to experience being human in a brand-new way. A way that isn't driven by habit, repetitive thinking, reliving the past, speculating about the future, or being paralyzed by the fear of change.

Consciousness is a way of living that focuses on an authentic experience of the moment, awareness of your truth, and the full comprehension that by choosing your reaction to every one of your experiences, you are creating your reality.

This book contains simple but powerful tools that will help you make the shift from the fear-based operating system (survival) to the consciousness-based operating system (fascination).

These tools can be used throughout your spiritual journey. They require no props, no rituals, no religious beliefs, and can be easily incorporated into your day-to-day activities. In addition, they build on one another and can be used in powerful combinations that will rapidly transform your experience.

The first section introduces 22 tools. The second section defines and clarifies nearly 100 terms and concepts. You can read this volume in any order. It is not a narrative, but a reference book you will likely turn to time and time again.

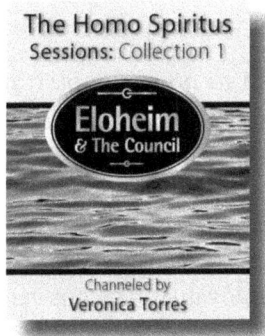

The Homo Spiritus Sessions, Collection One

COLLECTION ONE includes transcripts of EIGHT Eloheim and The Council channeling sessions held between July 7, 2010 and August 25, 2010.

It's not WHY is this happening? It's WOW this is happening! Experiences are here to facilitate growth, expansion, and transformation. Nothing happens TO you; it all happens FOR you. You create your reality by choosing your reactions to your experiences.

The spiritual journey is a natural process of expansion (growth) and contraction (contemplation). Through this process, you discover the truth of you and learn to emanate that truth into the world. Empower yourself by discerning the difference between vulnerability and weakness. Evolve your relationship to the survival instinct; don't let fear and habits tell you who you are!

The truth of you is emanated into the world through your choices about how you react to your creations. If issues come up again, it doesn't mean you're broken, it means you're going deeper.

Feelings are not emotions! Feelings are a deep and powerful pathway to ascension based on what is actually occurring in this moment. Emotions are habitually, biologically, and/or culturally based. Be vulnerable. Tell the truth. Be honest about your feelings. Be willing to admit when you want to learn something. Open to the fact that you don't know everything.

When you're tempted to be in the past or the future, we invite you to say: "Am I courageous enough to be with me now? Am I courageous enough to attend to my concerns about me, fascination with me, my insight about me? Am I courageous enough to do that?"

Where do you feel unlovable? The answer is the doorway to the next level of your spiritual growth. The true nature of your infinite, and immortal self resides just a breath away in any moment, and it exists for you to access at any time.

The Homo Spiritus Sessions series offers channeled messages from Eloheim and The Council.

The Council is comprised of seven different groups: The Guardians, The Girls, The Visionaries, The Matriarch, The Eloheim, The Warrior, and Fred. During a channeling session, each of The Council members take turns sharing their teachings. Each Council member has a distinct personality, style of delivery, and focus.

The Council is best known for their multitude of practical tools, which support our journey out of the fear-based operating system into the consciousness-based operating system.

COLLECTION ONE INCLUDES 29 TOOLS:

Big toe, left elbow; Choose and choose again; Color with all the crayons; Don't be mean to yourself; Equal signs; Feelings are not emotions; Feet under shoulders; Go to the bathroom; How ridiculous does it have to get?; Mad Scientist; Money mantra; Neutral observation; "No" is a complete sentence; Point fingers; Preferences/Judgments; Re-queue; Script holding; Short, factual statements; Velcro; Vulnerability vs. weakness; What is in your lap?; What is IS; What is true now?; Where am I lying to myself?;

Who answers the door?; Why, why, why?;Wow!, not why?; You can't have change without change; You to you (compare).

ADDITIONALLY, **COLLECTION ONE** INCLUDES **126** DEFINITIONS OF TERMS AND CONCEPTS.

Each of the *Homo Spiritus Sessions* books can stand alone, but taken together will allow the reader to follow along with the progression of the teachings including the introduction, in-depth explanation, and evolution of The Council's tools.

***

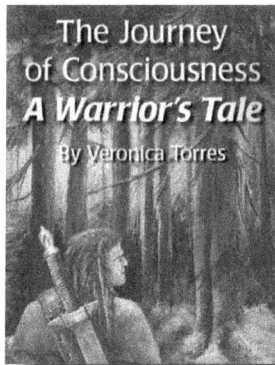

The Journey of Consciousness, A Warrior's Tale

"This entire story is to help you know who you are."

This "fairy tale for grown-ups" follows the Warrior's journey as he encounters castles and kings, battles and beasties, while learning to live from an open heart. The Warrior explains how to live the truth of you, how to have a healthy relationship to authority figures, and how to be vulnerable and strong at the same time.

"Anything that is presenting itself to you is presenting itself to you for growth."

Filled with humor, sage advice, penetrating insight, and above all, profound support for your process, the Warrior's tale clarifies your spiritual path.

"Now, it's really fun to see the King when you stink. Why? Because what you want the king to know is that you are not just a little pawn in his game to be manipulated to his benefit. When you go to see the king, whomever the king is in your world, take who you are with you, and if that means you drop mud on this perfect floor, well, there you are."

***

The Warrior is one of the seven Council members channeled by Veronica Torres. The Council's teachings focus on spiritual growth and the movement from the fear-based to the consciousness-based operating system. They specialize in offering specific tools which will facilitate your spiritual growth.

In addition to the Warrior's story, The Journey of Consciousness includes the following tools: Clarity vs. certainty; Feet under shoulders; How ridiculous does it have to get?; I don't know anything; Lay it down and walk away; Mad scientist; Neutral observation; "No" is a complete sentence; Point fingers; Preferences/judgments; Script holding/Script-holders; Strongest chakra; Vulnerability vs. weakness; What's in your lap?; What is true now?; Where am I lying to myself? "Wow!", not "why?", and You to you (comparing). It also includes 126 definitions of terms and concepts used in The Council's teachings.

***

"When you're facing your triggers, if you start to waiver in your courage, just imagine that we stand behind you. We stand there to show you that you don't have to fear that you are not enough. You can be afraid of the triggers, but don't be afraid that you're not enough. We will stand beside you in consciousness and courage any time you wish." – The Warrior

Eloheim and The Council books are available online through major book retailers and by visiting eloheim.com/dlg/cart/index.php.

www.ingramcontent.com/pod-product-compliance
Lightning Source LLC
Chambersburg PA
CBHW070535030426
42337CB00016B/2214